The Amber Nectar

WELCOME to the best and most comprehensive Whisky Cocktail Book from Scotland, the home of the Amber Nectar. As many of you will know the relationship between Whisky, the world's oldest spirit and Cocktails, the world's greatest party drink, is as old as the spirit itself. It is because of this unique relationship that this book was compiled, allowing the connoisseurs, to increase their party repertoire by adding Scotch Whisky, the water of life. This book not only opens up the world of whisky but will also revitalise your parties, making them and you 'The Talk of the Town'.

The Amber Nectar

The Magic of Whisky

Roger Hunter
and
Peter G. Hunter

LINDSAY PUBLICATIONS

First published in 2004 by
Lindsay Publications
Glasgow

© Roger Hunter and Peter G Hunter

ISBN 1 898169 31 4

The moral rights of the authors have been reserved

All rights reserved

No part of this publication may be reproduced, stored in a retrieval system, or transmitted in any form, or by any means electonic, mechanical, photocopying, recording or otherwise without the express permission of the Publisher

British Library Cataloguing-in-Publication Data
A Catalogue record of this book is available
from the British Library

Designed and typeset by Eric Mitchell
in Benguiat Book 10 point
Cover photograph by Martin W. Paul
www.photographyten.com

Printed and bound by Bell and Bain, Glasgow, Ltd

History

BEFORE WE DELVE into the delights of Whisky Cocktails, it is important to understand the history of both Cocktails and Whisky. Cocktails have been around since the 1700s, becoming an established drink in the 1800s. There are almost as many origins to the name as there are Cocktails but here are the most popular and likely of them all:

During the late 1760s, a non-thoroughbred horse was termed *cock-tailed* because it was of mixed blood. It is therefore possible that the term soon gained acceptance as a description for anything containing mixed fluids.

Another possibility also comes from the racing world. For a person or a horse to be *cock tailed* meant that they were of high spirits. Any drink, which therefore increases such high spirits, could conceivably have been called a cocktail.

In the 1700s a handsome soldier was once served a drink, which contained all the colours of a *cocks tail* whereby he immediately named it a cocktail.

A traditional French recipe for mixed wines was called a *coquetel*, which upon establishment in America, was transformed into the term cocktail.

Another possible French origin comes from Coquetier, the French term for eggcup. Legend has it that a Frenchman in New Orleans served mixed drinks from these eggcups and the term cocktail stems from these eggcups.

The history of Whisky is not as clouded. The first recorded reference to Whisky occurs in the 1400s but there is much evidence to suggest that whisky was introduced to the Highlands of Scotland as far back as the 800s. It is possible that the ancient Celts brought the technique of distilling grains from the Orient, via Spain and Europe and into Ireland. There is evidence of distilling in Ireland at the turn of the first millennium. In the 1200s when England invaded Ireland, they came across a barley spirit which had been heard of but neither seen nor tasted.

The most likely introduction of this famous spirit though is thought to be through Islay and Campbelltown, a well known route used by Holy men including St Columba. It is believed that it was the monks who introduced the art of distilling and during Medieval times abbeys were the centre of communities where learning, science, religion and the production of alcoholic drinks occurred.

The first recorded reference to distilling was in 1494 when an entry in the Exchequer Rolls lists 'Eight bolls of malt to Friar John Cor of Dunfermline wherewith to make aqua vitae'. This would have been enough to make approximately 1500 bottles of aque vitae, a sure sign that distilling was a well-established practice. This aqua vitae, which was later known in the Gaelic as *uisge beatha* is known today as 'the water of life', 'the amber nectar' or more simply, Scotch Whisky.

Contents

History   5

Equipment   9

Measurements   15

Chapter One   17

Cocktails you can make using only Whisky, Orange, Lemon, Lime, Grapefruit and Pineapple Juices, Powdered Sugar, Beer and some sprigs of mint.

Chapter Two   23

To the ingredients from Chapter One, add Ginger Ale, Soda Water and Cola.

Chapter Three   29

To the ingredients from Chapters One and Two add Milk, Eggs, Cream and a little Nutmeg.

Chapter Four   33

Add sweet and dry vermouth and a dash of grenadine to expand your cocktail cupboard.

Chapter Five 43

You need all the above and the additions of Benedictine and Angostura Bitters.

Chapter Six 53

These recipes are all non-alcoholic using the juices of Orange, Lemon, Lime, Grapefruit and Pineapple, Ginger Ale, Soda Water, Cola, Milk, Eggs, Cream, Nutmeg, Grenadine and Angostura Bitters.

Index 59

Equipment

THE EQUIPMENT available for making cocktails is wide and varied, but the essential equipment for Cocktail Magic is as follows:

- *Ice Bucket* classier and handier than having to grab ice from the freezer each time a guest wishes a drink.
- *Ice Scoop* a better alternative to picking ice up with your hands and one I'm sure your guests would appreciate.
- *Shaker* the capped variety comes with a built in strainer while the Boston Shaker consists of two flat-bottomed cones which fit neatly together. If using a Boston Shaker you will need a Hawthorn strainer.
- *Mixing glass* used to stir ingredients together. Ensure the Hawthorn strainer fits the mixing glass.
- *Hawthorn strainer* can be used to strain drinks from both the Boston Shaker and the Mixing Glass.
- *Long Handled Bar Spoon* essential for stirring drinks and ideal for layering drinks (see Tips).
- *Corkscrew* the best ones are the ones which actually spiral as opposed to the ones which don't.
- *Cocktail Sticks* available in wood or plastic.
- *Fruit Knife* for that all important slice of lemon or orange.

- **Straws** longs drinks should be served with straws.
- **Tea Towel** to ensure buffed and sparkling glasses.

Glassware

Although all cocktails have a recommended glass, there are no absolute rules. It may be unseemly to serve a martini in anything other than the classic cocktail glass but few people are likely to refuse the drink because it's in the wrong glass. Short of serving your drinks in a chipped coffee mug the following rules should help you out:

- *The best glasses should be thin lipped and of good quality.*
- *Glasses should be crystal clean to show the beauty of the cocktail. Fingerprints aren't attractive.*
- *The longer the drink, the taller the glass.*

Frosting & Chilling glasses

Some drinks call for the glass to be frosted or chilled. Here's how to do both:

- *Frosted Glass* Store in the freezer or bury in shaved ice long enough to give each glass a cold, frosted look and feel.
- *Chilled Glass* Place in the freezer long enough for it to go cold, alternatively fill with crushed ice a few minutes before using or fill with cracked ice and stir around the glass. When the drink is ready, empty the ice from the glass, shaking out the melted ice.

Ice

With ice you only need one thing – lots of it. Ice is a key ingredient for making cocktails and you will need more than you think. Ice can be the difference between a cool, swinging party which lives long in peoples memories and a damp squib where everyone leaves early to catch last orders at the local. To ensure you have the former, make your ice a couple of days before the party. Four people on a sunny evening could easily go through 2kg of ice whether it is Cubed, Cracked, Crushed or Shaved.

- *Cubed ice* can come in a variety of different shapes and sizes. Experiment with different moulds or try adding fruit for more fun.
- *Cracked ice* put the cubes in a freezer bag and hit with a rolling pin, against the wall or other suitably hard surface.
- *Crushed ice* basically the same process as cracked but with more effort. You want the ice crushed into small pieces.
- *Shaved ice* shaved ice is thin slivers of ice and cools a drink very quickly. An ice grater is ideal for making shaved ice. If you don't have an ice grater then use a normal grater or to save your grater batter the ice into really small pieces.

Sugar Syrup

Many recipes call for sugar syrup which sweetens cocktails and gives them body. Sugar does not dissolve easily in cold drinks but sugar syrup does. Sugar syrup can be made as follows:

Use a small saucepan and stir in 300ml (10fl.oz) of sugar with the same amount of hot water. Stir over a low heat till the sugar is dissolved. Make this up before the party and keep in a sterilised bottle in the fridge for up to 6 weeks.

Sweet and Sour

This is a key ingredient in your cocktail arsenal. Make Sweet and Sour Mix (also known as Sour or bar mix) as follows:

Mix one part heavy sugar syrup (3 parts sugar, 2 parts water) with one part lemon juice and add 2 egg whites per litre of mix. The egg whites are optional, but will make the drinks slightly foamy. You may want to adjust the sugar/juice ratio to give the mix the right balance of sweetness and tartness.

Handy Hints

Every good bartender has a few tricks up their sleeve which helps the party run smoothly. Here's some of the best ones:

Flaming Drinks: First of all ensure the top layer of the drink is 40%+ alcohol. Make sure it is near the rim of the glass and fill a metal (not a plastic) barspoon with the same liquid. Heat the barspoon with the flame from a lighter and when hot light the liquid in the spoon. Now place the spoon over the glass and impress your guests with a flaming drink. Make sure it doesn't burn too long in case the glass cracks or the rim becomes too hot. The glass must be placed on the table before you light it and *not* in your guest's hand. Flaming drinks can be very dangerous. If the party is outside, have a bucket of sand available. If it is inside then have a tub of baking soda available.

Champagne: Although it looks good when those on the winning podium shower everyone with champagne, your guests may not be as appreciating if you spray their clothes with the foaming bubbly. The best way to open champagne is to use a clean dish-towel. Place the top of the bottle in the middle of the dish-towel loosely wrapping the towel around the bottle. With one hand holding the dish towel and the bottle, use the other hand to slowly unscrew the cork. This should allow you to open the champagne without losing your precious bubbly.

Layering: Pour the liquor with the highest alcohol content into the glass first and then add the rest in descending order. When adding the rest of the liquors pour the liquor slowly over an upturned barspoon. The rounded barspoon will layer the liquor without it mixing, creating a very impressive effect.

Muddling: Some drinks call for ingredients to be muddled. To do this use the back of a spoon to crush the ingredients into a pulp. You can purchase a muddler specifically for the job and these are normally made out of wood.

Glasses: Test your glasses to establish how much liquid they can hold. Check them with crushed, broken and whole ice cubes and again use the measure to see how much fluid they will hold. This will let you know how much of each type of ice you need for drinks which are 2,3,4 or more measures in size. This will allow you to make a cocktail to fit the glass.

Twists: Many recipes call for a 'twist of lemon or orange'. To make a twist of any citrus fruit, cut a piece of peel from the fruit, squeeze the zest from the skin on top of the finished cocktail and drop the peel in the drink. Special tools can be used to create different effects such as spirals or zigzags but use your imagination.

Shaken or stirred?

James Bond, always deadly, always unique and only shaken when partaking of drink. Even when he drinks, Bond remains that little bit different from the rest of us. How? Well as a general rule, clear drinks, like martini, should be stirred, not shaken, while cloudy drinks, those with fruit juices for example, should be shaken, not stirred.

Shaker

A few handy hints for getting the best out your shaker:

Shake and Strain: Half fill shaker with ice cubes, add the ingredients and shake until the shaker is cold to the touch. Pour through the strainer, leaving the ice behind and a wonderfully cold drink in front.

Shake and pour: As above but without the straining. When doing this ensure you don't use too much ice or the glass will overflow when poured.

Drinks using crushed ice are intended to be unstrained.

Don't fill your shaker more than four-fifths full.

Never shake fizzy drinks.

Wash the shaker between different cocktails.

When using egg or cream give your shaker a thorough wash to get rid of any sticky residue.

Finally, remember that part of the appeal of cocktails is in the presentation, not just the taste. They should be pleasing to the eye as well as to the tastebuds. Serve your cocktails on a napkin and with a smile.

Measurements

In this book we use measures, teaspoons and dashes.

A measure is 25ml of fluid.

A teaspoon is a level teapoonful or approximately ⅙ of a measure.

A dash is ¼ of a teaspoonful unless a dash of egg-white which is one teaspoonful of egg white.

A splash is two drops of the appropriate liquid.

Remember that making a cocktail is not a science but an art. A cocktail does not depend on exact measurements but on the art of making a pleasing drink.

Now that you have the foundations in place, here are the cocktails.

Now that you have the foundations in place, here are the cocktails.

Dedication

This book is dedicated to Jamie
with love.

With special thanks to Carol and Beth,
whose cocktail antics and shenanigans
inspired this book.

Chapter One

A VARIETY of the cocktails you can make using only Whisky, Orange Juice, Lemon Juice, Lime Juice, Grapefruit Juice, Pineapple Juice, Powdered Sugar, Beer and some sprigs of mint. These are not only some of the easiest cocktails to make but they also rely on ingredients which anyone should be able to access quickly and cheaply. With these limited ingredients you should be able to make the following:

BOILERMAKER   *INK STREET*   *KING KOLE*
NEW YORKER   *SCOTCH ON THE ROCKS*
SCOTCH SOUR   *SCOTS MIST*   *WALTERS*
WHISKY FIX   *WHISKY SANGAREE*
WHISKY SLING   *WHISKY SMASH*

BOILERMAKER

1 msr Scotch Whisky
½ Pint of Beer

Any two drinks consisting of whisky and beer as a chaser creates a boilermaker.

Magic Fact: The BOILERMAKER is a classic that originated in the 1920s from the working class men of Scotland. This is a serious drink and not to be taken lightly. Allegedly Dylan Thomas, the famous Welsh poet drank these in New York. It is said that one evening he drank as many as twenty, stepped outside and died. This is possible – so beware.

Magic Fact: To create a DEPTHCHARGE, pour whisky into shot glass or measure, place a half pint glass over the top and turn quickly upside down. The whisky should now be sealed in by the shot glass. Keep your finger on the shot glass and slowly fill the ½ pint glass with beer. Now drink! The whisky should only be released as you near the end of the drink, providing a killer kick.

Note: Don't use plastic shot glasses for this. It won't work.

INK STREET

1 msr Scotch Whisky
1 msr Orange Juice
1 msr Lemon Juice

Shake all ingredients well with ice and strain into a cocktail glass. Decorate with a slice of orange and cherry if desired.

KING KOLE

2 msr Scotch Whisky
½ tsp Powdered Sugar
1 slice Orange
1 slice Pineapple

Muddle sugar, orange, and pineapple in a whisky glass. Add Whisky and 2 ice cubes. Stir well.

NEW YORKER

1 msr Scotch Whisky
1 tsp Lemon Juice
1 tsp Lime Juice
1 tsp Powdered Sugar

Shake all ingredients except the lemon juice with ice until a froth forms and strain into a cocktail glass. Pour the lemon juice over the surface and decorate with a twist of lemon peel.

Scotch on the Rocks
2 msr Scotch Whisky

Pour scotch into a whisky glass half filled with ice cubes. Nice, uncomplicated and tried and tested over the centuries.

Scotch Sour
2 msr Scotch Whisky
1 msr Lemon Juice
½ msr Sugar Syrup (*see instructions on page 00*)

Shake all ingredients well with ice and strain into whisky glass. Decorate with a twist of lemon peel.

Magic Fact: Sours were established around the 1850s being made with a little sweetener and a substantial amount of lemon juice, hence the name. The sugar syrup can be varied to suit individual tastes.

Substitute the following spirits to make a range of differing sours; 2 msr Vodka – Vodka Sour; 2msr Tequila – Tequila Sour; 2 msr Canadian Whiskey – Stone Sour; 1½ msr White Rum, ½ msr Golden Rum – Rum Sour; 2 msr Irish Whiskey – Irish Sour; 2 msr Southern Comfort – Southern Sour; 2 msr Bourbon – Bourbon Sour; 1½ msr Cherry Brandy – Cherry Sour; 1½ msr Apricot Brandy – Apricot Sour.

Scots Mist
2 msr Scotch Whisky

Shake briefly with a glassful of crushed ice, pour into a whisky glass and add a twist of lemon peel. Serve with a short straw for a more potent effect.

Magic Fact: replace Scotch with Gold Tequila to make Tequila Mist. Replace Scotch with Gin, Dark

Rum or Vodka and the twist of lemon with a twist of lime to make a GIN TWIST, RUM TWIST or RUSSIAN TWIST.

WALTERS

2 msr Scotch Whisky
½ msr Orange Juice
½ msr Lemon Juice

Shake all ingredients well with ice and strain into a cocktail glass to make this little poppet.

WHISKY FIX

2 msr Scotch Whisky
½ msr Sugar Syrup
Juice of ½ Lemon

Shake all ingredients well with ice and strain into a whisky glass part filled with crushed ice and decorate with orange, lemon or cherry.

Magic Fact: Fixes became popular in America in the early 1800s when the syrup was initially made from the fruit in season such as raspberries or strawberries.

Replace the Whisky with Bourbon, Brandy and Gin to make their respective Fixes and replace with 1 msr Dark Rum and 1 msr White Rum to make a RUM FIX.

WHISKY SANGAREE

2 msr Scotch Whisky
1 msr Sugar Syrup

Stir all ingredients in a whisky glass with crushed ice, sprinkle with ground nutmeg and decorate with a slice of lemon.

WHISKY SLING

2 msr Scotch Whisky
2 msr Cold Water
1 msr Sugar Syrup
1 msr Lemon Juice

Dissolve sugar syrup in water and lemon juice. Add whisky. Pour into a whisky glass over ice. Stir. and decorate with a twist of lemon peel.

Magic Fact: A sling was a device to handle barrels and the drinks were traditionally made with plain cold water. A sling should contain sugar syrup or a sweet liqueur instead and lemon or lime juice although any base spirit and fruit juice can be used. Substitute the Scotch with Bourbon, Brandy, Gin, Rum and Vodka to make their respective slings. Alternatively, try making your own using your own choice of spirit and fruit drinks.

WHISKY SMASH

2 msr Scotch Whisky
½ msr Sugar Syrup
4 sprigs Mint

Add the Sugar Syrup and the mint to a whisky glass and muddle the two together, ensuring the mint is well crushed. Add the whisky and fill with crushed ice, decorating with a cherry, slice of orange and a sprig of mint.

Magic Fact: The term 'smash' probably originates from the smashing of the ice and its first appearance occurs in the 1850s. Other popular smashes include the GIN, BRANDY and RUM SMASHES, where Gin, Brandy and White Rum replace the Whisky.

Chapter Two

WITH THE ingredients from Chapter One add Ginger Ale, Soda Water or Cola to make the following cocktails. These ingredients are readily available and are common ingredients for cocktail-making. These extra ingredients make the following:

CABLEGRAM *CANAL STREET DAISY*
HIGHLAND COOLER *HORSE'S NECK*
JOE COLLINS *KLONDIKE COOLER*
MAMIE TAYLOR *NERIDA* *SCOTCH AND SODA*
SCOTCH HIGHBALL *SCOTCH RICKEY* *SWEET AND SOUR*
WHISKY FIZZ *WHISKY MAC*

CABLEGRAM
2 msr Scotch Whisky
1 tsp Powdered sugar
1 msr Lemon Juice
Ginger Ale

Stir Whisky, Sugar and Lemon Juice with ice cubes in highball glass and fill with ginger ale.

CANAL STREET DAISY
1 msr Scotch Whisky
¼ msr Lemon Juice
¼ msr Orange Juice
Soda Water

Pour all ingredients, except the soda, into a Collins or tall glass over 2–3 ice cubes. Top up with soda water and decorate with a slice of orange.

Highland Cooler

2 msr Scotch Whisky
2 msr Soda Water
½ tsp Powdered Sugar

Dissolve powdered sugar in 2 msrs of soda water in a Collins or tall glass. Add scotch and several ice cubes and stir. Fill with soda water and stir again. Decorate with a twist of lemon or orange peel so that the ends dangle over the rim of the glass.

Horse's Neck

2 msr Scotch Whisky
Ginger Ale

Peel rind of whole Lemon in a spiral placing it in a Collins or tall glass with the end on the rim. Keeping the spiral on the rim of the glass, fill glass with ice cubes, add whisky, and fill with ginger ale stirring well.

Joe Collins

2 msr Scotch Whisky
5 msr Soda Water
1 msr Lemon Juice
1 tsp Sugar

Shake all ingredients except the soda water with cracked ice and strain over three ice cubes into a Collins or tall glass. Fill with soda water and stir gently. Decorate with slice of lemon, orange and a cherry.

Magic Fact: At the turn of the 1800s John Collins was a famous head waiter at *Limmers*, a hotel and coffee house in London. John Collins was his signature drink and Joe Collins is the Scottish version. This may also be known as a SCOTCH COLLINS or, if American Whiskey is used, a BOURBON COLLINS.

KLONDIKE COOLER

2 msr of Scotch Whisky
½ tsp of Powdered Sugar
1 spiral of Orange
1 twist of Lemon
Soda Water

Mix powdered sugar and 2 msr soda water in a Collins or tall glass. Fill glass with ice and add blended whiskey. Fill with soda water and stir. Decorate with a twist of lemon and orange peel so that the ends dangle over the rim of the glass.

MAMIE GILROY

3 msr Scotch Whisky
½ msr Lime Juice
Ginger Ale

Mix Scotch and lime juice in a Collins or tall glass filled with ice and stir. Top with ginger ale and stir again. Decorate with a slice of lemon.

NERIDA

3 msr Scotch Whisky
½ msr Lime or Lemon Juice
Ginger Ale

Shake all the ingredients with ice, except the ginger ale, and strain into a cocktail glass. Top up with ginger ale. Decorate with lemon or lime slices.

Scotch and Soda

2 msr Scotch Whisky
5 msr Soda Water

Pour scotch over one ice cube into Highball or tall glass. Add the Soda Water and decorate with a twist of lemon peel.

Scotch Highball

2 msr of Scotch Whisky
5 msr Ginger Ale or Soda Water

Pour Scotch in a highball or tall glass over ice cubes. Top up with the ginger ale or soda water and decorate with a twist of lemon.

Magic Fact: Highball probably comes from catering to railroad workers. A ball was raised on a high pole to tell and encourage passing train drivers to hurry up. With the speed at which this drink can be concocted, the term 'highball' came to represent a drink which could be made and drunk by railroad workers in a very short period of time.

Scotch Rickey

2 msr Scotch Whisky
4 msr Soda Water
½ msr Lime Juice

Use a Collins or tall glass and pour lime juice onto one ice cube, add the scotch, stir and add the soda water. Decorate with a wedge of lime.

Magic Fact: Rickeys first arrived on the cocktail scene in 1893 when a Congressional Lobbyist, Joe Rickey, was made a cocktail of spirit, lime juice and soda water. The most famous Rickey is the Gin Rickey which can be made by substituting the

Scotch for the Gin, as can the BOURBON RICKEY, BRANDY RICKEY, SLOW GIN RICKEY, VODKA RICKEY and RUM RICKEY.

SWEET AND SOUR

1 msr of Scotch Whisky
2 msr of Sweet and Sour *(see instructions page 12)*
Cola

Pour scotch and sweet and sour into a Collins or tall glass over ice cubes and stir well. Fill with cola and stir lightly. Decorate with a cherry.

WHISKY FIZZ

1½ msr Scotch Whisky
2 msr Lemon Juice
½ msr Sugar Syrup
Soda Water

Shake all ingredients with ice, except the soda water, and strain into Highball or tall glass filled with ice. Top up with soda water and decorate with a slice of lemon.

WHISKY MAC

1 msr Scotch Whisky
1 msr Ginger Ale

Using a whisky glass, pour the whisky and ginger ale over two ice cubes. Stir briefly and serve.

Magic Fact: This can also be made using Ginger Wine for a more potent cocktail.

Chapter Three

ADD Milk, Eggs, Cream (preferably double and whipped) and a little Nutmeg from your spice rack to the ingredients from the previous chapters to make the following party essentials.

Boston Sour *Cowboy* *Derby Fizz*
Hot Scotch *Irish Coffee* *Whisky Flip*
Whisky Milk Punch *White Plush*

Boston Sour
2 msr Scotch Whisky
1 msr Lemon Juice
½ msr Sugar Syrup
1 Egg White

Shake all ingredients well with ice and strain into a cocktail glass.

Cowboy
2 msr Scotch Whisky
1 tbsp Double Cream

Shake all ingredients well with cracked ice and strain into a cocktail glass.

Derby Fizz
2 msr Scotch Whisky
1 msr Lemon Juice
½ msr Sugar Syrup
1 Egg
Soda Water

Shake all ingredients well with ice, except the soda water, and pour into a Highball or tall glass. Top up with soda water and stir.

Hot Scotch
4 msr Scotch Whisky
1 tsp Powdered Sugar
Hot Water
Nutmeg

Dissolve the sugar in a few drops of water. Add Scotch. Fill with hot water, then decorate with twist of lemon peel and finally top with nutmeg. A nice little number after being out in the cold.

Irish Coffee
2 msr Scotch Whisky
5 msr Black Coffee
1½ msr Whipped Cream
1½ tsp Powdered Sugar

Pour whisky into a coffee cup. Add sugar and fill with hot, black coffee. Stir to dissolve sugar. Float whipped cream on top, do not stir. Decorate with a straw if desired.

Magic Fact: The original recipe first appeared after World War II. Since then, adding ½ msr Kahlua has become very fashionable and using Irish Whiskey adds a more authentic flavour.

Whisky Flip
2 msr Scotch Whisky
½ msr Sugar Syrup
1 Egg (beaten)

Shake all ingredients well with ice and strain into a cocktail glass, sprinkling with grated nutmeg.

Magic Fact: Flips got their names from being flipped back and forth between two containers, normally a Boston Shaker, which consists of two flat-bottomed cones which fit neatly together.

Flips have been around since the 1600s and have changed considerably throughout that period, initially having warm ale as an ingredient. Flips can be made with egg, sugar syrup and any type of liquor. Basically, if it's a liquor, it can be a Flip. Use 2 msrs of Vodka for a VODKA FLIP, 2 msrs of Southern Comfort for a COMFORTABLE FLIP, 2 msrs of Brandy for a BRANDY FLIP and so on.

WHISKY MILK PUNCH

2 msr Scotch Whisky
3 msr milk
1 msr Sugar Syrup
Grated nutmeg

Shake all ingredients well with ice until a froth appears and strain into a Collins or tall glass. Sprinkle with grated nutmeg and serve.

WHITE PLUSH

2 msr Scotch Whisky
5 msr Milk
1 tsp Powdered Sugar.

Shake all ingredients well with ice and strain into a Collins or tall glass.

Chapter Four

TO EXPERIMENT with the following recipes, add the essentials of sweet and dry vermouth and a dash of grenadine to expand your cocktail cupboard.

(Remember French Vermouth is *dry*, Italian Vermouth is *sweet*. Neither do well if left too long in an opened bottle so refrigerate after opening).

Magic Point: Many experts differed on the use of sweet or dry vermouth in the following cocktails. The best solution is to experiment and go with what you like. Cocktails which are not the exact recipe but which taste good are better than exact recipes which taste bad!

ADDINGTON	ALGONQUIN	ARROWHEAD
BEADLESTONE	BEALS	CLEAR SKIES AHEAD
CRYSTAL BRONX	HALF AND HALF	HARRY LAUDER
JUMBO	KARL K KITCHEN	LOS ANGELES
MANHASSET	MANHATTAN	MIAMI BEACH
MICKIE WALKER	NEW WORLD	NEW YORK COCKTAIL
OPENING	SKIPPER	TENNIS GIRL
THE CROW	VERMOUTH COCKTAIL	
VICTORY	WARD EIGHT	WEMBLEY
WHISKY SPECIAL	WHISKY SQUIRT	WHISPER COCKTAIL
WILD IRISH ROSE	WOODWARD	

ADDINGTON

2 msr Sweet Vermouth
2 msr Dry Vermouth
Soda Water

Stir all ingredients, except the soda water, and strain into glass. Top up with soda water.

ALGONQUIN

3 msr Scotch Whisky
1 msr Dry Vermouth
1 msr Pineapple Juice

Stir juice, vermouth and whisky with ice until nearly frothing, then strain into chilled cocktail glass.

ARROWHEAD

1 msr Scotch Whisky
1 tsp Dry Vermouth
1 tsp Sweet Vermouth
1 tsp Lemon Juice
1 Egg White

Shake all ingredients well with ice and strain into a cocktail glass.

BEADLESTONE

2 msr Scotch Whisky
2 msr Dry Vermouth

Stir with ice and strain into cocktail glass.

BEALS

2 msr Scotch Whisky
2 msr Dry Vermouth
2 msr Sweet Vermouth

Stir with ice and strain into cocktail glass.

CLEAR SKIES AHEAD

2 msr Scotch Whisky
1 Egg White
½ msr of Lemon Juice
½ msr Grenadine
½ tsp of Sugar Syrup

Shake all ingredients well with ice until a froth forms then pour into a chilled whisky glass.

CRYSTAL BRONX

2 msr Dry Vermouth
2 msr Sweet Vermouth
2 msr Orange Juice
Soda Water

Pour ingredients over ice in a Collins or tall glass and top with soda water.

Magic Fact: When served with a slice of orange this is called a WYOMING SLING.

HALF AND HALF

2 msr Dry Vermouth
2 msr Sweet Vermouth

Pour ingredients over ice in a whisky glass and decorate with a twist of lemon.

HARRY LAUDER

2 msr Scotch Whisky
2 msr Sweet Vermouth
2 dashes Sugar Syrup

Shake all ingredients well with ice and strain into a cocktail glass.

JUMBO

1 msr Scotch Whisky
1 msr Dry Vermouth
1 msr Sweet Vermouth

Shake all ingredients well with cracked ice and strain into a cocktail glass.

KARL K KITCHEN

3 msr Scotch Whisky
1 msr Grapefruit Juice
4 dashes Grenadine

Shake all ingredients well with ice and strain into a cocktail glass.

LOS ANGELES

2 msr Scotch Whisky
¼ msr Sweet Vermouth
½ msr of Lemon Juice
1 tsp Powdered Sugar
¼ Egg (beaten)

Shake all ingredients well with cracked ice and strain into a whisky glass.

MANHASSET

2 msr Scotch Whisky
1½ msr Dry Vermouth
1½ msr Sweet Vermouth
1 msr Lemon Juice

Shake all ingredients well with cracked ice and strain into a cocktail glass.

MANHATTAN

3 msr Scotch Whisky
1 msr Sweet Vermouth

Stir vigorously with ice then strain into a chilled cocktail glass. Decorate with a cherry and serve.

Magic Hint: Like many other drinks of its time, the much-favoured vermouth is key in the cocktail. In the past the measures of vermouth outnumbered that of whisky by 2:1 however this has somewhat decreased as a result of changing tastes. With all cocktails there is no defining ratio, it is all down to personal taste but we recommend the ratio of 3:1 in favour of whisky. The substitution of whisky with Brandy or Rum will create their respective Manhattans. The substitution of Southern Comfort for whisky creates the COMFORTABLE MANHATTAN.

MIAMI BEACH

2 msr Scotch Whisky
2 msr Dry Vermouth
1 msr Grapefruit Juice

Shake all ingredients well with cracked ice and strain into a cocktail glass.

MICKIE WALKER

3 msr Scotch Whisky
1 msr Sweet Vermouth
1 dash Lemon Juice
1 dash Grenadine

Shake all ingredients well with ice and strain into a cocktail glass.

New World

2 msr Scotch Whisky
½ msr Lime Juice
1 tsp Grenadine

Shake all ingredients well with cracked ice and strain into a whisky glass filled with crushed ice.

New York Cocktail

2 msr Scotch Whisky
½ msr Lime Juice
½ tsp Powdered Sugar
1 dash of Grenadine

Shake all ingredients well with cracked ice and strain into a cocktail glass.

Opening

2 msr Scotch Whisky
1 msr Sweet Vermouth
1 tsp Grenadine

Shake all ingredients well with cracked ice and strain into a chilled cocktail glass.

Skipper

3 msr Scotch Whisky
1 msr Dry Vermouth
½ msr of Orange Juice
4 drops Grenadine

Pour the grenadine over ice and add orange juice, vermouth and whisky. Stir vigorously, until nearly frothy, and pour into glass. Decorate with a slice of orange.

TENNIS GIRL

1 msr Scotch Whisky
2 msr Sweet Vermouth
1 dash Lime Juice

Shake all ingredients well with ice and strain into a cocktail glass.

THE CROW

½ msr Scotch Whisky
1 msr Lemon Juice
1 dash of Grenadine

Shake all ingredients well with ice and strain into a cocktail glass.

VERMOUTH COCKTAIL

2 msr Sweet or Dry Vermouth
1 dash Angostura Bitter

Shake all ingredients well with ice and strain into a cocktail glass.

VICTORY

1½ msr Dry Vermouth
1½ msr Sweet Vermouth
¼ msr Lemon Juice
¼ msr Orange Juice
2 dashes Grenadine

Shake all ingredients well with ice and strain into a cocktail glass.

WARD EIGHT

2 msr Scotch Whisky
½ msr of Lemon Juice
1 tsp Powdered Sugar
1 tsp Grenadine

Shake all ingredients well with cracked ice and strain into a wine glass. Decorate with orange and lemon slices.

Magic Fact: The WARD EIGHT hails from Locke-Ober Café in Boston where patron Martin Lomasney was running for office in 1898. Bartender, Patrick Fogarty concocted it on the eve of the election and named it after Lomasney's election Ward number.

WEMBLEY

1 msr Scotch Whisky
1 msr Dry Vermouth
1 msr Pineapple Juice

Shake all ingredients well with ice and strain into a cocktail glass.

WHISKY SPECIAL

3 msr Scotch Whisky
2 msr Dry Vermouth
½ msr Orange Juice
Nutmeg

Shake all ingredients well with ice and strain into a cocktail glass. Add a little nutmeg and serve with an olive or cherry.

WHISKY SQUIRT

1 msr Scotch Whisky
1 tbsp Powdered sugar
1 tbsp Grenadine
Soda Water

Shake all ingredients except soda water with ice and strain into a Highball or tall glass. Fill with soda and ice cubes. Decorate with a slice of pineapple and after strawberry pieces.

WHISPER COCKTAIL

1 msr Scotch Whisky
1 msr Dry Vermouth
1 msr Sweet Vermouth

Shake all ingredients well with ice and strain into a cocktail glass.

WILD IRISH ROSE

2 msr Scotch Whisky
2 msr Soda Water
¾ msr Lemon Juice
½ msr Grenadine

Fill Highball or tall glass with ice. Add all ingredients except soda water and stir. Fill with soda water.

WOODWARD

2 msr Scotch Whisky
½ msr Dry Vermouth
1 tbsp Lemon or Grapefruit Juice.

Shake all ingredients well with ice and strain into a cocktail glass.

Chapter Five

FOR THESE recipes, you need all the previous ingredients and the cheeky additions of Benedictine and Angostura Bitters for you to make:

AFFINITY	*BENEDICT*	*BENOLA*
BOBBY BURNS	*BRAINSTORM*	*CLUB*
FLYING SCOTSMAN	*FRISCO SOUR*	*HILDERBRANDE*
HOLE IN ONE	*HOOTS MON*	*HOT TODDY*
JUNIOR	*LOCH LOMOND*	*MANHATTAN DASH*
MANHATTAN DASH (DRY)		*OH HENRY*
OLD-FASHIONED	*PALMER*	*PERFECT ROB ROY*
PREAKNESS	*ROB ROY*	*SOUTHGATE*
STONE FENCE	*THE PERFECT MANHATTAN*	
THISTLE	*TWIN HILLS*	*WHISKY BOMB*
WHISKY COCKTAIL	*WHISKY SWIZZLE*	*WIDOWS DREAM*

AFFINITY

1 msr Scotch Whisky
1 msr Dry Vermouth
1 msr Sweet Vermouth
2 dashes Angostura Bitter

Put all the ingredients into a mixing glass with ice cubes. Stir and strain into cocktail glass.

BENEDICT

3 msr Scotch Whisky
1 msr Benedictine
Dry Ginger Ale

Put the ice cubes into mixing glass. Pour Benedictine and whisky over the ice. Stirring evenly and without straining pour cocktail into highball or tall glass. Top up with ginger ale.

Magic Fact: Benedictine has been produced by the Benedictine monks since the early sixteenth century. Made from a secret recipe, it includes aromatic herbs and spices.

BENOLA

2 msr Benedictine
4 msr Cola

Half fill whisky glass with ice, add the benedictine, then the cola, stir and decorate with a slice of lemon.

BOBBY BURNS

1 msr Scotch Whisky
1 msr Dry Vermouth
1 tsp Benedictine

Shake all ingredients well with cracked ice until a froth forms and strain into a chilled cocktail glass. Decorate with a twist of lemon peel.

Magic Fact: This cocktail is dedicated to none other than Robert Burns (1759–96). Scotland's most famous poet and songwriter is remembered each year on the 25th January, where the traditional meal of haggis, neeps and tatties is served along with gallons of Scotch Whisky. His most famous song would probably be classed as that of *Old Lang Syne*, a traditional song used to bring events such as Weddings and Ceilidhs to an end.

BRAINSTORM

2 msr Scotch Whisky
2 dashes Dry Vermouth
2 dashes Bendictine

Put all the ingredients into a mixing glass with ice cubes. Stir and strain into cocktail glass. Decorate with a cherry.

CLUB

1 msr Scotch Whisky
2 dashes Angostura Bitter
1 dash of Grenadine

Put ice into mixing glass. Add the bitters then the whisky and grenadine. Stir well before straining into cocktail glass. Decorate with a twist of lemon and a cherry.

FLYING SCOTSMAN

1 msr Scotch Whisky
1 msr Sweet Vermouth
1 dash Angostura Bitter
¼ msr Sugar Syrup

Put all the ingredients into a mixing glass with ice cubes. Stir and strain into cocktail glass.

FRISCO SOUR

2 msr Scotch Whisky
½ msr Benedictine
½ msr of Lime Juice
¼ msr of Lemon Juice

Shake all ingredients well with ice and strain into a whisky glass. Decorate with a slice of lemon and lime.

HILDERBRANDE

2 msr Scotch Whisky
2 dashes Angostura Bitter
1 tsp sugar
Sprig of Mint

Muddle sugar and bitters in a whisky glass. Add ice, twist of lemon peel, slice of orange and a sprig of mint, before pouring in the scotch. Serve with a smile!

HOLE IN ONE

2 msr Scotch Whisky
1 msr Sweet Vermouth
1 dash Lemon Juice
1 dash Angostura Bitter

Shake all ingredients well with ice and strain into a cocktail glass.

HOOTS MON

2 msr Scotch Whisky
¼ msr Sweet Vermouth
1 tsp Benedictine

Put all the ingredients into a mixing glass with ice cubes. Stir and strain into cocktail glass. Decorate with a twist of lemon peel dropped into the glass.

Magic Fact: *Hoots Mon* is a traditional Scottish greeting meaning *Hallo Man*.

HOT TODDY

2 msr Scotch Whisky
4 msr Boiling Water
3 drops Angostura Bitter
1 slice Lemon
1 tsp Sugar (*preferably brown*) or Honey

Combine ingredients together adding the sugar or honey last. Stir well and sprinkle a little ground nutmeg on top. Adding a cinnamon stick is a nice little extra. This drink is commonly used to soothe the throat from a harsh cold, or perhaps just another excuse to have a drink when you're ill.

Magic Fact: In Edinburgh, during the 1600 and 1700s, *Tods Well* was an essential source of water for the city. During this period, the Hot Toddy was as essential in surviving the harsh Scottish winters as the well was in providing the water which went with it. In fact, the Hot Toddy can be made with any spirit and should have spices, a little sweetener and citrus fruit to go with it.

Junior

2 msr Scotch Whisky
2 tsp Lime Juice
2 tsp Benedictine
2–3 dashes Angostura Bitter

Shake all ingredients well with cracked ice and strain into a cocktail glass.

Loch Lomond

1 msr Scotch Whisky
1 tsp Sugar Syrup
2 dashes Angostura Bitter

Shake ingredients with ice and strain into a cocktail glass.

Manhattan Dash

2 msr Scotch Whisky
1 msr Sweet Vermouth
1 dash Angostura Bitter

Shake all ingredients well with ice and strain into a cocktail glass. Decorate with a cherry.

Manhattan Dash (Dry)

2 msr Scotch Whisky
¾ msr Dry Vermouth
1 dash Angostura Bitter

Put all the ingredients into a mixing glass with ice cubes. Stir and strain into a cocktail glass. Decorate with an olive or twist of lemon.

Oh Henry

½ msr Scotch Whisky
½ msr Benedictine
½ msr Ginger Ale

Shake all ingredients well with ice and strain into a cocktail glass.

Old-Fashioned

2 msr Scotch Whisky
1 tsp Water
2 dashes Angostura Bitter
1 Sugar Lump

In a whisky glass muddle sugar, bitters and water until sugar has dissolved. Add one ice cube, Scotch and a twist of lemon peel. Add soda water if desired. It depends on whether you like a fizzy drink or not! Stir well. Decorate with a slice of orange and a cherry and serve with a stirrer.

Palmer

2 msr Scotch Whisky
1 dash Angostura Bitter
½ tsp Lemon Juice

Put all the ingredients into a mixing glass with ice cubes. Stir and strain into cocktail glass.

PERFECT ROB ROY

2 msr Scotch Whisky
½ msr Sweet Vermouth
½ msr Dry Vermouth

Put all the ingredients into a mixing glass with ice cubes. Stir and strain into a cocktail glass. Decorate with a twist of lemon.

PREAKNESS

2 msr Scotch Whisky
1 msr Sweet Vermouth
1 tsp Benedictine
1 dash Angostura Bitter

Put all the ingredients into a mixing glass with ice cubes. Stir and strain into cocktail glass. Decorate using a twist of lemon peel.

ROB ROY

1 msr Scotch Whisky
½ msr Dry Vermouth
1 dash Angostura Bitter

Put the ice cube, whisky, vermouth and bitters into mixing glass and stir well. Strain into a cocktail glass and decorate the rim with a twist of lemon peel.

Magic Fact: This variation of The Manhattan is named in honour of the seventeenth-century, legendary Scottish thief and hero, Rob Roy MacGregor.

Roy is the Scottish colloquial term for a man with red hair, the colour of this drink.

Southgate

2 msr Scotch Whisky
½ tsp Sugar Syrup
2–3 dashes Angostura Bitter

Shake all ingredients well with cracked ice and strain into a cocktail glass. Decorate with a twist of lemon peel.

Magic Fact: It is unsure about the origin of this drink, but it does not have anything to do with the England penalty miss against Germany in the semi-finals of Euro 1996.

Stone Fence

2 msr Scotch Whisky
2 dashes Angostura Bitter
Soda Water

Pour scotch and bitters over an ice cube into a whisky glass and top up with soda water.

The Perfect Manhattan

2 msr Scotch Whisky
1 msr Sweet Vermouth
1 msr Dry Vermouth
1 dash Angostura Bitter

Put all the ingredients into a mixing glass with ice cubes. Stir and strain into cocktail glass. Decorate with a cherry.

Thistle

2 msr Scotch Whisky
2 msr Sweet Vermouth
2 dashes Angostura Bitter

Put all the ingredients into a mixing glass with ice cubes. Stir and strain into cocktail glass.

Twin Hills

2 msr Scotch Whisky
2 tsps Benedictine
1½ tsp Lemon Juice
1½ tsp Lime Juice

Shake all ingredients well with ice and strain into a whisky glass. Decorate with a slice of lime and lemon.

Whisky Bomb

2 msr Scotch Whisky
¼ msr Sugar Syrup
2 dashes Angostura Bitter

Put all the ingredients into a mixing glass with ice cubes. Stir and strain into a cocktail glass.

Whisky Cocktail

2 msr Scotch Whisky
1 tsp Sugar Syrup
1 dash Angostura Bitter

Put all the ingredients into a mixing glass with ice cubes. Stir and strain into cocktail glass. Decorate with a cherry.

Whisky Swizzle

2 msr Scotch Whisky
1 msr Lime Juice
1 tsp Sugar
2 dashes Angostura Bitter
Soda Water

Put lime juice, sugar and a small amount of soda water into Collins or tall glass. Fill glass with ice and stir. Add bitters and whisky. Fill to top with soda water and serve with a swizzle stick.

Widows Dream

1 msr Benedictine
1 Egg
Double Cream

Shake all ingredients with ice, except the cream, and strain into a cocktail glass. Layer cream on top.

Chapter 6

NON-ALCOHOL COCKTAILS

AS GREAT AS cocktails are, the non-alcohol cocktail is an essential to make sure a party goes swingingly well. The days of having 'one for the road' are thankfully gone. For you to be a responsible and excellent host, you need to cater for all your guests; that includes those who aren't drinking. This selection of cocktails are formed from the ingredients found in previous chapters and will ensure you can be the perfect host to every one of your guests by offering them one of the following:

BORA-BORA CINDERELLA LIME COOLER
NO RUM RICKEY ORANGE AND TONIC
PAC-MAN PINK LEMONADE POMOLA
PUSSYFOOT ROY ROGERS SHIRLEY TEMPLE
SOUTHERN GINGER SPARKLING LEMONADE
SPARKLING LIMEADE SPARKLING ORANGEADE
STILL LEMONADE TEQUILA SUNSET VIRGIN MARGARITA

BORA-BORA

3 msr Pineapple
3 msr Ginger Ale
½ msr Grenadine
1 tsp Lime Juice

Shake all ingredients with ice, except the ginger ale, and strain into a Highball or tall glass. Top up with ginger ale and decorate with a cherry, a slice of lime and a straw.

CINDERELLA

2 msr Orange Juice
2 msr Pineapple Juice
1 msr Lemon Juice
½ msr Sugar Syrup
1 msr Soda Water

Shake all ingredients with ice, except the soda water, and strain into a Highball or tall glass. Add the soda water and decorate with a slice of lemon and a straw.

LIME COOLER

Cola
1 dash of Lime Juice

Pour the cola into a Highball or tall glass half filled with ice cubes. Add the dash of lime juice, decorate with a lime slice and serve.

NO RUM RICKEY

1 msr Lime Juice
2 dashes Angostura Bitter
2 dashes Grenadine
Soda Water

Shake all ingredients well with ice, except the soda water, and strain into a Highball or tall glass. Top up with soda water and decorate with a slice of lime.

ORANGE AND TONIC

4 msr Orange Juice
Tonic Water

Pour the orange juice into a Highball or tall glass half filled with ice cubes. Top up with tonic water and decorate with a slice of orange.

Pac-Man
1 dash of Lemon Juice
1 dash of Angostura Bitter
1 dash of Grenadine
Ginger Ale

Pour the lemon juice, angostura bitter and grenadine into a Highball or tall glass half filled with ice cubes. Top up with ginger ale and decorate with a slice of orange.

Pink Lemonade
1½ msr Lemon Juice
1½ msr Sugar Syrup
⅓ msr Grenadine
4 msr Cold Water

Shake all ingredients well with ice and strain into a Highball or tall glass. Decorate with a slice of lemon, a cherry and a straw.

Pomola
1 msr Lime Juice
5 msr Cola
⅓ msr Grenadine

Fill glass with ice, add all the ingredients and decorate with a slice of lemon, a cherry and a straw.

Pussyfoot
3 msr Orange Juice
¼ msr Lemon Juice
¼ msr Lime Juice
1 Egg Yolk
1 dash Grenadine

Shake all ingredients well with ice and strain into a cocktail glass.

Roy Rogers

1 dash of Grenadine
Cola

Pour the grenadine into a Highball or tall glass half filled with ice cubes. Top up with cola and decorate with a cherry.

Shirley Temple

1 msr Grenadine
Ginger Ale

Fill Highball or tall glass with ice and pour in the grenadine. Top up with ginger ale, stirring all the time and decorate with a straw.

Southern Ginger

5 msr Ginger Ale
1 sprig of mint
½ msr Sugar Syrup
½ msr Lemon Juice

Muddle the mint in the glass and fill with crushed ice. Add all the ingredients and stir, serving with a straw.

Sparkling Lemonade

1½ msr Lemon Juice
1½ msr Sugar Syrup
4 msr Soda Water

Shake all ingredients well with ice, except the soda water and strain into a Highball or tall glass. Add the soda water and decorate with a slice of lemon and a straw.

SPARKLING LIMEADE

1½ msr Lime Juice
1½ msr Sugar Syrup
4 msr Soda Water

Shake all ingredients well with ice, except the soda water, and strain into a Highball or tall glass. Add the soda water and decorate with a slice of lemon and a straw.

SPARKLING ORANGEADE

1½ msr Orange Juice
1½ msr Sugar Syrup
4 msr Soda Water

Shake all ingredients well with ice, except the soda water, and strain into a Highball or tall glass. Add the soda water and decorate with a slice of orange and a straw.

STILL LEMONADE

1½ msr Lemon Juice
1½ msr Sugar Syrup
4 msr Cold Water

Shake all ingredients well with ice and strain into a Highball or tall glass. Decorate with a slice of lemon, a cherry and a straw.

TEQUILA SUNSET

6 msr Orange Juice
1 dash of Grenadine

Pour the orange juice into a Highball or tall glass half filled with ice cubes and add the dash of grenadine.

Magic Fact: Ironically, this non-alcohol version of the Tequila Sunrise will allow you to face the sunrise in the morning bright eyed and bushy tailed.

Virgin Margarita
2 msr Lime Juice
1 msr Lemon Juice
1 msr Orange Juice
½ msr Sugar Syrup

Shake all ingredients well with ice and strain into salt rimmed cocktail or margarita glass.

All 155 Cocktails in Alphabetical order

Addington 34
Affinity 43
Algonquin 34
Apricot Sour 19
Arrowhead 34

Beadlestone 34
Beals 34
Benedict 43
Benola 44
Bobby Burns 44
Boilermaker 17
Bora-Bora 53
Boston Sour 29
Bourbon Collins 24
Bourbon Fix 20
Bourbon Rickey 26
Bourbon Sling 21
Bourbon Sour 19
Brainstorm 45
Brandy Fix 21
Brandy Flip 30
Brandy Manhattan 37
Brandy Rickey 26
Brandy Sling 21
Brandy Smash 22

Cablegram 23
Canal Street Daisy 23
Cherry Sour 19
Cinderella 54
Clear Skies Ahead 35
Club 45
Comfortable Flip 30
Comfortable Manhatten 37
Cowboy 29
Crystal Bronx 35

Depthcharge 17
Derby Fizz 29

Flying Scotsman 45
Frisco Sour 45

Gin Fix 20
Gin Mist 19
Gin Rickey 26
Gin Sling 21
Gin Smash 22

Half and Half 35
Harry Lauder 35
Highland Cooler 24

Hilderbrande 46
Hole in One 46
Hoots Mon 46
Horse's Neck 24
Hot Scotch 30
Hot Toddy 46

Ink Street 18
Irish Coffee 30
Irish Sour 19

Joe Collins 24
Jumbo 36
Junior 47

Karl K Kitchen 36
King Kole 18
Klondike Cooler 25

Lime Cooler 54
Loch Lomond 47
Los Angeles 36

Mamie Gilroy 25
Manhasset 36
Manhattan 37
Manhattan Dash 47
Manhattan Dash (*Dry*) 48
Miami Beach 37
Mickie Walker 37

Nerida 25
New World 38
New York Cocktail 38

New Yorker 19
No Rum Rickey 54

Oh Henry 48
Old-Fashioned 48
Opening 38
Orange and Tonic 54

Pac-Man 55
Palmer 48
Perfect Rob Roy 49
Pink Lemonade 55
Pomola 55
Preakness 49
Pussyfoot 55

Rob Roy 49
Roy Rogers 56
Rum Fix 20
Rum Manhattan 37
Rum Mist 20
Rum Rickey 26
Rum Sling 21
Rum Smash 22
Rum Sour 19
Russian Mist 20

Scotch and Soda 26
Scotch Collins 24
Scotch Highball 26
Scotch on the Rocks 19
Scotch Rickey 26
Scotch Sour 19
Scots Mist 20

Shirley Temple 56
Skipper 38
Slow Gin Rickey 26
Southern Ginger 56
Southern Sour 19
Southgate 50
Sparkling Lemonade 56
Sparkling Limeade 57
Sparkling Orangeade 57
Still Lemonade 57
Stone Fence 50
Stone Sour 19
Sweet and Sour 27

Tennis Girl 39
Tequila Mist 20
Tequila Sour 19
Tequila Sunset 57
The Crow 39
The Perfect Manhattan 50
Thistle 50
Twin Hills 51

Vermouth Cocktail 39
Victory 39
Virgin Margarita 58
Vodka Flip 30
Vodka Rickey 26
Vodka Sling 21
Vodka Sour 19

Walters 20
Ward Eight 39
Wembley 40
Whisky Bomb 51
Whisky Cocktail 51
Whisky Fix 20
Whisky Fizz 27
Whisky Flip 30
Whisky Mac 27
Whisky Milk Punch 31
Whisky Sangaree 21
Whisky Sling 21
Whisky Smash 22
Whisky Special 40
Whisky Squirt 40
Whisky Swizzle 51
Whisper Cocktail 41
White Plush 31
Widows Dream 52
Wild Irish Rose 41
Woodward 41
Wyoming Sling 35

www.cocktailmagic.com

The Only Place for All Your Cocktail Requirements.

We can provide you with
Party Cocktail Kits
Ice Buckets
Shakers
Pourers
Glasses
Jiggers
And a Cocktail of other essentials!

Cocktail Magic.com
Putting the Magic Back into Cocktails